Victoria, B.C. Travel Guide

Sightseeing, Hotel, Restaurant & Shopping Highlights

James Crawford

Copyright © 2014, Astute Press
All Rights Reserved.

No part of this publication may be reproduced, stored in a retrieval system, or transmitted, in any form or by any means without the prior written permission of the publisher, nor be otherwise circulated in any form of binding or cover other than that in which it is published and without similar condition being imposed on the subsequent purchaser.

If there are any errors or omissions in copyright acknowledgements the publisher will be pleased to insert the appropriate acknowledgement in any subsequent printing of this publication.

Although we have taken all reasonable care in researching this book we make no warranty about the accuracy or completeness of its content and disclaim all liability arising from its use

Table of Contents

Victoria, B.C. 5
    Culture 6
    Location & Orientation 8
    Climate & When to Visit 8

Sightseeing Highlights 10
    Butchart Gardens 10
    Discovery Island 12
    Victoria Bug Zoo 14
    Beacon Hill Park 15
    Royal British Columbia Museum 17
    Pacific Undersea Gardens 18
    Afternoon Tea at the Empress Hotel 20
    Craigdarroch Castle 21
    Maritime Museum of British Columbia 23
    Chinatown 24
    Inner Harbor 25
    Vancouver & Seattle 25

Recommendations for the Budget Traveler 27
    Places to Stay 27
        Howard Johnson City Center 27
        Gatsby Mansion Inn 28
        Rosewood Inn 29
        Spinnakers Brew Pub & Guest Houses 30
        HI-Victoria Hostel 32
    Places to Eat & Drink 33
        John's Place 33
        ReBar 33
        Dutch Bakery 34
        BC Legislative Dining Room 35
        The Mint 36
    Places to Shop 37
        Government Street Market 37
        Munro's Books 38
        Ditch Records 39
        Silk Road Tea 40

Victoria, B.C.

Victoria is the capital of British Columbia and is situated to the south of Vancouver Island off the west coast of Canada. Victoria, B.C. is a small, beautiful "Garden City" known for its impressive Butchart Gardens and other parks. The city has the world's most northerly Mediterranean climate.

Victoria may not have a hockey team and artists will probably play at venues in Vancouver. International flights will passby overhead. But these are minor matters. Victoria is a worthy stop in its own right.

First of all, it's not nearly as crowded as its more famous neighbor. The surrounding mountains are among the most beautiful in the world. The native population had life relatively easy. With the abundance of wildlife and fish they did not have to toil their days away looking for food. With their leisure time they created art. The richness and splendor of indigenous art is not found until you reach the Huichols of central Mexico.

All manner of outdoor activities are just a drive away. Vancouver is so close that you could easily drive there, spend the day seeing the city and take in a show or a hockey game and get back to where you're staying for the night. Seattle is only 74 miles or 119 kilometers away. Better yet, the Victoria Clipper is a high-speed catamaran that runs daily back and forth between Victoria and Seattle. This ride will take you past the San Juan Islands. The waters around the islands are the hunting and breeding grounds for Killer Whales. It is not uncommon to see a pod making its way up the sound.
http://www.clippervacations.com/

Culture

Victoria is the capital city of British Columbia. It was named, not surprisingly, after Queen Victoria. It originally began as a trading post in the mid-19th century. With money came people and the city was established. It is one of the oldest cities in the Pacific Northwest.

As the city grew it originally was intended to be a taste of home for British expats. For a long while it was dubbed the most British city outside of Great Britain. Travelers today would be a bit hard pressed to see the resemblance as it has taken a decided turn toward the modern. Still much of the old intentions remain. When every street corner on earth has a coffee shop planted on it, Victoria still observes teatime. The British love of gardens was transplanted and took to new heights. Indeed, the city is known as "The City of Gardens." Victoria's love for its gardens is matched only by the Japanese. One garden in particular, Butchart Garden, must be included in every discussion of the most beautiful gardens in the world.

While the area surrounding Victoria has grown to accommodate a burgeoning population, the bulk of the city itself was built before WWI. Beautiful as Vancouver may be, its skyline has an eerie resemblance to Hong Kong. Not so with Victoria. The old style architecture and lack of the hustle and bustle found in its more famous neighbor make Victoria a perfect place to stroll and soak up the atmosphere.

While it is not the big name draw Vancouver is, Victoria is not a cultural backwater. It has its own symphony and ballet company. An electronic music festival is held yearly. While still observed, exclusiveness of teatime has given way to accommodate the upscale restaurants, wine shops and brew pubs that dot the city. Victoria is a popular location for movie shoots. Movies such as 'X-Men' and 'Final Destination' were shot here. Television shows such as 'Smallville' and 'The Dead Zone' were filmed in and around the city.

Location & Orientation

Victoria actually is a city on an Island. It is the southernmost city of Vancouver Island. To the east the Cascade mountain range and the Canadian Rockies converge. The Canadian Rockies are one of the world's great mountain ranges rivaling those found in Switzerland and the Himalayas. On its doorstep are the waters of Puget Sound and The Strait of Juan de Fuca. The dividing line between the United States and Canada runs along the Strait of Juan de Fuca.

Commercial marine traffic coming to Canada and the United States are met at the mouth of the Strait of Juan de Fuca. Here professional pilots will board and steer the craft to whatever ports it is going to on Puget Sound. Across the strait is the U.S. city Port Angeles. Beyond this is the Olympic mountain range. As you travel north from Victoria you will some of the lushest and most pristine pine forests in the world. Farther north still and you will meet the border of Alaska to the west. At this point you are in the desolate and forbidding Yukon which continues on to the Arctic Ocean.

Climate & When to Visit

Looking at a map might give a person the impression that it is too far up there to be much fun. Surprisingly, however, Victoria has a very mild climate. Weather fronts have some pretty impressive mountain ranges to deal with leaving Victoria in a bit of a rain shadow. Vancouver is an hour's drive away yet it receives almost three times as much rain as Victoria.

The winter months can be rainy though snow is very rare. Winter high and low temperatures range between 8 and 4 C (46 and 39F). Spring time highs will be 11-18C (51-64F) and the lows between 6-8C (37-46F). Summers are very sunny and pleasant. Daytime highs range between 19-20C (66-68F) and lows between 10-11C (50-51F). In autumn the highs start at about 17C and get down to 11C (62-51F).

http://www.victoria.ca/index.html?sredir=1
http://www.tourismvictoria.com/

Sightseeing Highlights

Butchart Gardens

800 Benvenuto Ave.
Central Saanich, BC
V8M IJ8 Canada
866-652-4422
http://www.butchartgardens.com/index.php?option=com_frontpage&Itemid=1

Butchart Gardens (Pronounced butch-art) is simply one of the most beautiful gardens in the world.

People will drive from as far away as Seattle just to spend an afternoon at the gardens before heading home. Work on the garden began in 1907 when Robert Pim Butchart commissioned Isaburo Kishida from Yokohama Japan to begin designing the garden. Within a few years work on the original garden was complete and more flora and fauna was added. In 1926 the Butchart family opened the gardens to the public.

Today the public gardens are contained within a 55 acre area. The rest of the gardens, which are off limits to tourists, are used for a variety of purposes. Six greenhouses are used to propagate and maintain the high quality of plants found on its grounds. The gardens are open year round but there are a couple of peak growing seasons. One is in the spring and the remaining two in summer. Winter is the low season but plants that thrive this time of year can be seen. The website is most helpful and has a link that will tell you what is blooming week by week.

Butchart gardens are 23km (14 miles) north of Victoria. Buses running from Victoria and Vancouver will take you there. Victoria is also accessible by boats running from Vancouver and Seattle. Flights of floatplanes from Seattle also land nearby.

The gardens are open every day of the year at 9 a.m. except for Christmas day when they open at 1 p.m. Rates vary throughout the year, as well as by age and if you are part of a tour group. Check their website to see what applies to you.

Discovery Island

http://www.env.gov.bc.ca/bcparks/explore/parkpgs/discovery_is/
http://www.discoveryisland.ca/

If you look at a map of Victoria you will see Discovery Island just off its southeastern most point. It is an unspoiled bit if land. The island was 'discovered' by sailors aboard the HMS Discovery, a ship captained by George Vancouver. The larger island took the Captain's name while the small one was named after the boat.

Discovery Island is a very popular day trip. It is accessible only by boat. One of the more popular ways to visit the island is by sea kayak. Surrounding the island are the majestic San Juan Islands.

At the eastern end of the island are Sea Bird Point and its lighthouse. Sea Bird Point's name has nothing to do with the sea birds whirling overhead. Instead it was named, yet again, after a boat. In 1858 the American paddle steamer Sea Bird was paddling in the waters nearby when it caught fire. To save the crew from a hideous death, the captain ordered the boat be run aground. All the crew members leapt to the safety of sea and land and the boat, its name and its ashes, were committed to eternity.

The Island did have one resident; Captain E. G. Beaumont who purchased part of the island in 1918. Captain Beaumont died in 1967. In 1972 the island was designated as a park. Captain Beaumont was quite a colorful character. Right up to his death he would spend his time walking the length and breadth of the island and sailing the waters around it. The trails he padded are still in use today.

As of this moment, a healthy and hungry wolf prowls the island. If you are planning a visit in the near future you are not allowed to bring pets or food that is not cached. How *a* wolf got there is anybody's guess, but the island belongs to the critters and we humans must take a distant back seat. If you wish information on this or any other matters concerning the park, contact the BC Parks Area Supervisor at 250-391-2315.

The northern portion of the island is Indian reserve lands and off-limits to non-native visitors. Please respect this while visiting.

The park has a picnic area and a pit toilet. There is no running water on the island. Camping is permitted on parts of the island. The rules are very strict - if you packed it in, pack it out. If you're camping, leave no trace of your presence behind. Fires are strictly prohibited. Fishing is allowed on and around parts of the island. Make sure you are fishing in a spot designated for it and that you have the proper license.

Victoria Bug Zoo

631 Courtney Street
Victoria, BC V8W
Canada
250-384-2847
Mon-Fri 11 am to 4 pm, Sat and Sun 11 am to 5 pm
http://www.bugzoo.com/

Now here's a zoo worth visiting. Instead of looking at animals wandering in a pretend land or watching marine animals perform vaudeville acts, bugs don't ask much out of life and are usually quite happy right where they are. Victoria's bug zoo is home to some of the rarest insects in the world. Where else could you see a White-eyed Assassin Bug or a scorpion that glows-in-the-dark? If it creeps and crawls you're sure to find it slithering around the bug zoo.

The zoo has an ant farm that is quite fascinating to watch. A recent addition is Pharnacia, a bug that looks like a stick but can grow the length of your arm. One lucky visitor was there and saw a pair of mantis mating. She wrote in the visitor's book with great awe and envy how she watched the female eat her gentleman suitor.

Bugs are the things phobias and nightmares are made of. Yet to get down and see the world at their level is as close to visiting another planet as we earthlings will get. A visit here is well worth it. The Victoria Bug Zoo also makes great conservation and preservation efforts. Just visiting its website and links is a wonderful way to get to know a world around us that we seldom take the time to see.

Beacon Hill Park

James Bay, Victoria, BC
Canada
http://www.beaconhillpark.ca/

In keeping with the nautical theme, Beacon Hill is named for the two beacons on the hill that warned sailors that they in trouble. The waters around Vancouver Island can be treacherous. Rocky shoals seemingly pop out of nowhere. In some parts where land meets sea the land will drop quickly to a navigable depth while in others sharp rocks stretch out for quite a distance, hidden by the green water of Puget Sound. To warn sailors that they were headed into treacherous water, two beacons were planted atop a hill. One was a blue triangle and the other a green square. If a sailor could look through the triangle and see the square behind it he knew that he had to act quickly or the ship would run aground.

Today the park is a favorite of locals and tourists alike. It has a well-deserved reputation as the crown jewel of Vancouver's parks. The official web link is provided above. However, if you type the park into a search engine and look around, you will find that people quickly run out of superlatives when describing it.

The park itself is huge. In addition to wide open spaces and nature walks, it also has a soccer field. Situated within the park are a number of entertaining diversions. The Beacon Hill Children's Farm is a wonderful place to bring the kids. Here you will find a wide variety of birds and beasts. The purpose of the Children's Farm is to foster a love of animals. Children are to come away with a lifelong respect for nature's abundance.

The park is a haven for nature lovers. Birds, including Blue Herons and Bald Eagles, fly overhead. Deer, otters and raccoons scurry about while seals and sea lions swim in the waters. This part of the world is not often thought of as a mecca for scuba diving. The waters of Puget Sound are green because they are full of algae, the first rung on the food chain.

If you can brave the cold water you will find the diving to be stunning. The world's largest octopuses make their home here. The genuinely ugly wolf eel can be seen poking its menacing but harmless head out of nooks and crannies. Pods of killer whales are frequently seen as they make their way up and down the Sound. In the distance are the San Juan Islands, the snow-capped Mt. Baker and the jagged peaks of the Olympic Mountain range.

One of the great attractions is the Luminara Festival. Held each September from the 18th to the 25th, the festival plays host to some of the most creative luminara you will ever see. It bills itself as a "Festival of Light" and it truly is. Look around the internet for pictures and videos of this event.

Royal British Columbia Museum

675 Bellville St.
BC V8W 9W2
Canada
250-356-7226
http://royalbcmuseum.bc.ca/

What makes the Royal British Columbia Museum a worthwhile visit is its emphasis on the native culture of this part of Canada. The archeological museum has 192,000 artifacts with only 1% of them devoted to European and American items. Some of these artifacts date to the first people who ever visited this area. It is thought that Asia and North America were once connected by what is known as the Bering Land Bridge. This is thought because of some striking similarities between Asian artifacts and those found among the first settlements in the Americas. Artifacts from that period on up to the not too distant past are on display.

Earlier mention was made of the fact that the indigenous people of this area had plenty of food and were free to spend their leisure time in artistic pursuits. In the Ethnology museum you will find a rich mine of artifacts from Canada's indigenous people. A small number of objects are on display in the museum proper. The bulk of the objects are somewhat off limits to the public. The Ethnology Museum is generally used by scholars and artists but if you are interested in visiting you can schedule an appointment. It is asked that you give as much time as possible when scheduling your visit. It's advised that you read up a little to better appreciate what you are looking at. If you do visit you will be treated to some of the most beautiful works of art, crafts and adornment outside of Europe's finest museums.

In addition to the attractions, the museum also houses an IMAX theater. Movies are shown most every night. These include Hollywood films and documentaries. The emphasis is on shows of an educational nature. The museum prides itself on being a center of learning and its IMAX Theater reflects this. Movies change frequently. Check ahead to see what is playing while you are there.

The museum also has a webcam which you can visit to get a glimpse of this beautiful city:
http://royalbcmuseum.bc.ca/web-cam/

Pacific Undersea Gardens

490 Bellville St.
Victoria, BC
V8V 1W9
Canada
250-382-5717
http://www.pacificunderseagardens.com/

In a city that's known as the 'City of Gardens' it is appropriate that it has an undersea garden. If you'd "like to be beneath the sea in an octopus's garden in the shade" then you've found your aquatic Abby Road. Tropical reefs get all the ink but they are concentrated little cities outside of which nothing goes. Compared to Puget Sound, the waters found in tropical resorts are relative deserts. Marine life thrives in this nutrient rich water. An afternoon at the Pacific Undersea Gardens is the only way to get up close and personal with the marine life without getting wet.

What makes this garden unique is that it has been specially designed to accommodate the marine life. Visitors get aboard a boat that dives to a depth of 15 feet. This boat will then pass along the garden. Scuba divers equipped with radios and microphones will communicate with you telling you what you are seeing.

Fish such as salmon, perch and cod are apt to swim by. Giant starfish sit as if glued. Look around the internet for speeded up videos of starfish. In their way they are scurrying around and are voracious. When you see just how furiously they are moving and how ravenous their appetites are, you will these seemingly stationary and harmless creatures all the more. Beautiful anemones will be feeding on the plankton. Crabs will walk around looking for food and trying to avoid wolf eels and octopus. Clams will be siphoning the water trying to avoid starfish.

The ability to look beneath the water of Puget Sound is something you should take advantage of. To miss it would be a bit like going to Switzerland and not seeing the Alps.

Afternoon Tea at the Empress Hotel

721 Government St.
Victoria, BC
V8W 1W5
Canada
1-866-540-4429
http://www.fairmont.com/empress-victoria/

Later there will be a section on lodgings for the budget minded traveler.

The Empress Hotel will not be a part of it. It is consistently rated as one of the best hotels in the world. Words like sumptuous and palatial barely do it credit. It is a masterpiece of Victorian Architecture. Situated on the banks of the inner harbor, the Empress is the image that comes to mind when most people think of Victoria. It is as iconic a hotel to Victoria is as the Taj Mahal Palace is to Mumbai and the Frontenac Hotel is to Quebec City.

Through the years the Empress has had some notable people stay at it. Rudyard Kipling was a frequent guest. Shirley Temple stayed there amid rumors that she fled California to avoid being kidnapped. In 1939 King George VI and Queen Elizabeth dined at the hotel as guests of the Canadian government. The hotel is said to be a hotbed of hauntings. Through the years numerous ghost sightings have been reported.

What makes the hotel special for the casual visitor is its famous afternoon tea. During the summer months, afternoon tea is served in the Tea Room. The Tea Room can accommodate 800 people and it is packed. Tea is served along with tea sandwiches, scones and clotted cream. If you are planning on tea at the empress you must book well in advance. At least two weeks' notice is required. Tea costs $60 Canadian.

Craigdarroch Castle

1050 Joan Crescent
Victoria, BC
V8S 3L5
Canada
250-592-5323
http://www.thecastle.ca/

The motto in real estate is "location, location, location." When you're the wealthiest man in Canada you can afford to build a castle on the best location around. This is just what Robert Densmuir, a Scotsman who came to Canada and made his fortune in coal, did between 1887 and 1890. Unfortunately for Robert he fell over dead in 1889. Fortunately for his wife Joan, she inherited it and lived there until her death 20 years later.

If you had to pick the perfect spot for a house, or a castle, you would build it exactly where Densmuir did. It sits atop a hill that overlooks the city of Victoria. From the front you can look down upon Puget Sound as it snakes its way towards Seattle. To the east are the San Juan Islands.

Farther east are the rolling hills of the Cascade Mountains and the snowcapped volcano Mt. Baker. Victoria is where Puget Sound makes a dogleg, becomes the Strait of Juan de Fuca and connects with the Pacific Ocean. Beyond the Strait of Juan de Fuca are the rugged mountains of the Olympic Range.

The castle is as beautiful inside as it is outside. Densmuir spared no expense and furnished the castle with the latest and greatest in furniture and art. 120 years later the castle is a time capsule of Victorian era furnishing. Once you are in the castle you are free to begin your self-guided tour. If you're lucky enough to visit on a clear day, be sure to climb the 87 steps to the tower where you can enjoy the view.

In the 'City of Gardens' it's no surprise that Craigdarroch Castle has a garden that mirrors the buildings beauty. What makes this garden interesting is that it, like the castle's interior, the garden has remained as it was when it was built and acts as a snapshot of what the taste and style of gardens were at the turn of the century.

Maritime Museum of British Columbia

28 Bastion Square
Victoria, BC
V8W 1H9
Canada
250-385-4222
http://mmbc.bc.ca/

The Maritime museum is a fascinating look at the maritime history of this Island city. The first floor is devoted to the people who explored this area. From the indigenous population to Captains Cook and Vancouver, to the tug-of-war that took place in this area between Russia and the United States.

The second floor is devoted to models. Among the models is the HMS Nile built by prisoners of war in 1810. The models are extraordinary for the detail. They are obviously labors of love and are exquisite. The third floor was a courtroom. For a while it was where the Supreme Court sat. Today it has been restored to what it once was and is a fascinating look at courtrooms of old. Other exhibits tell the story of the Canadian Coast Guard and detail the Chinese laborers who arrived here looking for work in Canada and the States. Currently the museum is collecting and housing debris from the Japanese tsunami that is just now starting to wind up on the beaches.

Chinatown

In 1858 gold was discovered in the Fraser Valley. With gold comes a gold rush and people rushed to this area from all around the world. In particular they flooded in from Asia. As the gold rush subsided the people began to look for work elsewhere, most notably building the railways of Canada and the United States. As they made their way up and down the West Coast they established enclaves where they could retain their ways, language, and lifestyle. The largest and oldest of these Chinatowns is in San Francisco. Next in line is Victoria.

In the early part of the 20th century, it had a colorful if not notorious, reputation. It was a thriving boomtown and the population of Chinatown rivaled that of Victoria. Whispers and rumors had it that it was a place where opium dens thrived, ladies of the evening plied their trade and gambling establishments ran 24/7. Undoubtedly there was some truth to this but it is unlikely Chinatown harbored more dens of iniquity than any other part of Victoria.

By the middle of the century Chinatown fell into a stark decline. It has only been in the past 20 years that it has rebounded, dusted off and polished to its former glory. It makes a fascinating stroll. Walking down the narrow Tan Fan Alley it is easy to imagine shady goings on. Another point of interest is the entrance. Recently built this gate, known as 'The Gate of Harmonious Interest,' is as beautiful as it is ornate.

Inner Harbor

The Inner harbor is a beautiful walk that winds its way along the waterfront and past some of the city's main attractions. It's the perfect spot to watch the ship traffic heading in and out of the Pacific Ocean. Within walking distance are the Parliament Buildings, BC Museum and the Empress hotel.

The Empress is particularly beautiful on a warm summer night. The walk is home to a wide variety of colorful characters that sell all manner of merchandise, play all types of music and do what street performers the world over do. Along the Inner Harbor are places where you can rent a kayak and explore Victoria from Puget Sound. No matter what time of the day it is you will find many places to satisfy your hunger and thirst.

Vancouver & Seattle

Vancouver and Seattle are major cities that are within easy reach from Victoria. Vancouver is 94 km or 50 miles to the north. There are no convenient bridges that take you in that direction. The only way to get to Vancouver is by boat. Ferry boats run frequently between the two cities. You can either walk or drive. Busses in Vancouver are frequent and will take you anywhere you want to go. A day trip is possible but it is advised that spend at least a night in Vancouver to get an appreciation of the city.

To get to Seattle also requires you take a boat. You can either take a ferry to Anacortes Washington and drive three hours down Interstate 5 or you can take the passenger only catamaran known as the Victoria Clipper. The boat ride will take just under three hours and you will disembark at the north end of the city. Like Vancouver, the bus service in Seattle is outstanding. You may need a cab to get where you're staying but once you've dropped your bags off, the city as easily accessible by bus.

A rather exotic way of getting to Seattle is via floatplane. The plane leaves the Victoria harbor and lands 45 minutes later in Lake Union which is adjacent to the East end of Seattle. The company that operates these flights, Kenmore Air, also flies to other places in Canada and the San Juan Islands. If you would like to see this scenic part of the world from the air, this is how to do it.

Recommendations for the Budget Traveler

Places to Stay

Howard Johnson City Center

4670 Elk Lake Drive, Victoria, BC, V87 5M2
Canada
250-300-4656
http://www.hojovictoria.ca/

Conveniently located and surprisingly affordable, the Howard Johnson is the third most popular hotel in the city.

Its 80 rooms are all non-smoking. Each room is equipped with free Wi-Fi, an iron and ironing board, a microwave, refrigerator, air-conditioning, a coffee maker and hair dryer. The hotel has a pool, sauna and fitness center. A restaurant is on site that serves breakfast, lunch and dinner. Pets are allowed for a fee. The hotel is within ten minute driving distance from all the cities major attractions. The airport is a half hour away. Check-in is at 3 pm and checkout is 11 am. Rooms start at $66.

Gatsby Mansion Inn

309 Belleville St.
Victoria, BC
V8V 1X2
Canada
250-388-9191
http://www.bellevillepark.com/accommodation-gatsby.php

Located in the center of Bellville Park, the Gatsby Mansion Inn is a beautiful Victorian style mansion that has been converted into an inn. Among its numerous attractions is that it is within walking distance of where the Victorian Clipper docks and many other attractions listed above.

The inn has three levels of suites. The Main House which is the mansion, the Middle House and the Judges House. All of the rooms are non-smoking. Built over 100 years ago, the grounds of the inn reflect Victorian's love of gardening. Sumptuous, well-tended gardens bloom alongside waterfalls.

All of the rooms come with an alarm clock radio. Each room has a television with internet access. There is a telephone from which local and long distance calls can be made (A surcharge applies). Amenities such as a coffee maker, toiletries, and an iron and ironing board are included. Room service is available during limited hours. A laundry facility is available. Two restaurants are on site.

Rooms start at $99 per night

Rosewood Inn

595 Michigan St.
Victoria, BC
V8V 1S7
Canada
800-444-6633
http://www.viresorts.com/resorts/Rosewood.html

Billed as the 'City of Gardens Rosewood Inn,' this quaint stop is located in central Victoria. Built over 150 years ago, the inn was intended to make homesick travelers from Great Britain feel at home. Of its many attractions, what they are most proud of is just how British the inn and its surroundings resemble those found in the British Isles. Folks from Great Britain might not find this the getaway vacation they were looking for but it really is a charming location. Nearby attractions include Thunderbird Park and the Parliament buildings of this capital city.

The rooms are decorated with Victorian style furnishing. All rooms are smoke free. Included is maid service, cable TV, and free W-Fi. Complimentary tea is served in the morning. The inn also serves as your one-stop shop for all the tourist information and booking that you will need. From here you can book an afternoon of fishing, a scuba diving excursion, tickets to all the performances and museums. You can rent bikes and kayaks. Golfers can book a round at one of the local courses. You can book a three hour excursion on a tall ship.

Rooms start at $129 per night.

Spinnakers Brew Pub & Guest Houses

308 Catherine St.
Victoria, BC
V98 3S8
Canada
877-838-2739
http://www.spinnakers.com/

Right or wrong, the folks of the northwest corner of the United States and Canada pride themselves on being the epicenter of the microbrew and brew pub revolution. With this in mind it is appropriate to include an accommodation that is "within crawling distance" of one of Victoria's finer brew pubs.

Spinnakers is yet another accommodation built in the late 1800's and was intended to give the expat community the feeling that they were back home. The rooms are gorgeous and elegantly furnished. Three options are available. The 1884 Heritage Guest House consists of 5 guest rooms. Each room has 9 foot ceilings and wood floors. To relax and unwind you can choose between a tub with soaker jets or a steamer shower. Each room has a flat screen TV, free Wi-Fi, and a fireplace. There is a patio where you can sit outside and take in the view. If you're travelling to Victoria with that someone special, this is your best option in the city. If you have friends in tow you may want to book a room at the Garden Suites. It too has what the Heritage House has and a kitchen as well. The suites are a little larger and can hold up to 4 people. The Bungalow is, well, a bungalow. The bungalow sits amid the gardens in the back of the establishment. It comes with everything the other suites do only this one is kid and pet friendly.

All of the rooms have breakfast and fresh squeezed orange juice delivered to your door. Each room includes complimentary beer and truffle tasting.

The main attraction is Spinnakers Castro Brew Pub. It specializes in serving local cuisine and beer from its brewery and spirits from James Bay and Vic West.

With rooms starting at $239 per night, Spinnakers may be at the high end of the budget minded traveler's budget. But even budget minded travelers need to indulge in a bit of luxury now and again. Sometimes a quaint and cozy room that's "within crawling distance" from a class A brew pub is just the order to fill the bill.

HI-Victoria Hostel

516 Yates St.
Victoria, BC
V8W 1K8
Canada
250-385-4511
http://www.hihostels.ca/westerncanada/166/HI-Victoria.hostel

This is the backpacker's paradise. The Hi-Victoria is another in a chain of trusted hostels. Somehow these low rent hostels always seem to find themselves in a high rent district. The Hi-Victoria is no different. For the younger crowd with stronger legs, all of Victoria's sites are relatively nearby. The waterfront is a five minute walk away. The hostel itself is situated between the Parliament buildings and the Royal British Columbia Museum. Among its features are free internet access, a TV room and library, pool tables, a communal kitchen with microwave ovens and a laundry facility.

As is common with hostels, the Hi-Victoria is staffed by a knowledgeable crew. If you need information concerning Victoria and Vancouver you will have all your questions answered. If you're headed across Canada or down into the States, they will get you headed in the direction you need to go. Canada is an expensive country. To find a room at $23 per night in the heart of one of its most beautiful cities is the steal and deal of a lifetime.

Places to Eat & Drink

John's Place

723 Pandora Ave.
Victoria, BC
Canada
250-389-0711
http://www.johnsplace.ca/

John's Place bills itself as the perfect stop for the budget traveler and this is true. Open for breakfast, lunch and dinner every night of the week, John's Place meals are plentiful and delicious. John's Place is nothing fancy. Rather it is a good old fashioned diner. It's a place to get some chow, or grub. Breakfast can be pancakes, corned beef hash, huevos rancheros, etc. Lunch is burgers, sandwiches and salads. Diners are burgers, tortellini, fish and chips and shepherds pie. The southwestern meatloaf is a particular favorite. Dinners cost between $7 and $17.

ReBar

50 Bastion Square
Victoria, BC, Canada
250-361-9223
http://rebarmodernfood.com/

No sense in trying to create some hype. It's best to simply let the folks at ReBar tell you about themselves. "Fusing hippie-chic neo-noir retro-fitted coolness, this place brought together the best of the best: Healthy, delicious food in a trendsetting atmosphere."

That alone should merit a peek inside. However the tongue twister of a mission statement comes as advertised.

To quote them once again, "Refusing to embrace space-aged foods engineered to mimic freshness, ReBar has always celebrated real, local food." And that is what you'll get. Produce and herbs come from local farms. All the food is fresh and prepared on the spot. Nothing comes out of a box or a can. The ReBar is primarily a vegetarian restaurant though meat and seafood dishes are available. Be warned, the ReBar is one of the most popular restaurants in Victoria and the tables are often full. There is a reason for this. When you're in Victoria be sure to dine at the ReBar at least once. You will be glad you did.

Dutch Bakery

718 Fort Street
Victoria, BC
Canada
250-385-1012
http://thedutchbakery.com/

The Dutch Bakery wouldn't know what hippie-chic and neo-noir are if they were the only things that stood between them and grim death. This is baked goods from the old country. The Dutch Bakery has been in business for 60 years. It is extremely popular with Victorians who stop in for something to eat on or order baked goods for special occasions.

It's open Monday thru Saturday 7:30 am to 5:30 pm. While it's famous for its baked goods the restaurant is equally popular. The usual items like hamburgers and sandwiches can be had but it is the traditional Dutch meals that are the best. A particular favorite is their croquettes. Centrally located, the Dutch Bakery is the perfect place to take a break from sightseeing, have a pastry and tea and plan the rest of your day. Pastries are less than $2 and a sandwich or burger average $6.

BC Legislative Dining Room

501 Bellville St.
Room 606
Victoria, BC
V8V 2L8
Canada
250-0387-3959

When you scan the internet and travel books looking for places to eat, you will always find the BC Legislative Dining Room mentioned. Invariably at some point you will be told it is one of Victoria's "best kept secrets." How could still be secret it could possibly be is a matter of some doubt but the uniformity of reviews earns it a spot on our list with the caveat that the BC Legislative Dining Room is one of Victoria's best kept secrets.

True to the droll formality of governmental writing, the BC Legislative Dining Room is exactly that- the dining room of the BC legislative building. Located in the Parliament building, the dining area is where government employees come to eat. Getting to the restaurant is a lot less like walking into an eatery and more like being taken to an interrogation room.

Your journey will take you past security guards, check points and military personnel. Once inside you will be glad you were let in on this best kept secret.

Politicians sure know how to eat and the food here is five-star. Executive Chef Brian Vickstrom oversees the preparation of the meals. His pride in his craft and his attention to detail result in meals you will find in the swankiest and most upscale of restaurants.   Lunches cost between $6 and $16 and outside of the BC Legislative Dining Room, the quality of the meals served here are found at places where a glass of water will set you back $6. Only cash is accepted.

The Mint

1414 Douglas St.
Victoria, BC
V8W 2H1
Canada
http://themintvictoria.com/home

For those moments when only Tibetan and Nepalese food will do, you have The Mint in your corner. While traditional west coast food can be found here, this is the place where you can slake your craving for Badam Sandheco, Choyela and Goat Curry. For desert you can order Galub Jamun and relax the night away sipping on local beers and wine. The Mint opens for lunch at 10am and closes at 4pm. It reopens at 5pm and remains open until 2am. If your ventures have taken you late into the night or you've just returned from an event in Vancouver, The Mint is a great place to eat and take a bit of a walk on the exotic side. Meals range between $8 and $18.

Places to Shop

Government Street Market

1710 Government St.
Victoria, BC
V8W 1Z5
Canada
250-590-5379
http://www.pin.ca/market/

Open every day of the week from noon to 6pm, the Government Street Market is a bustling hive of activity. Shoppers jostle with street performers and musicians. The variety of items sold is staggering. If you can stick it in a bag and walk away with it you will most likely find a vendor at the street market selling it. If you wake up one morning and have an urge to purchase a didgeridoo or feel that only a pillow stuffed with buckwheat husks will provide the sleep you need, you can purchase it at the market. The market is the perfect place to browse, shop and purchases that something you will put on your mantle and, years later, wonder whatever on earth possessed you to buy it.

Munro's Books

1108 Government St.
Victoria, BC
V8W 1Y2
Canada
888-243-2464
http://munrobooks.com/

Founded by Jim Munro and bestselling author Alice Munro, Munro's books has been in business for 50 years. The building was built in 1909. It's exterior and interior are worth a look as it is considered one of the finest buildings in Victoria. The staff likes to point out that the 24 foot ceiling closely resembles that found at the library of Ephesus in ancient Rome.

All manner of books and genres can be found, but what the store is most noted for is its selection of modern literature. The staff is particularly knowledge in current literature. If you're looking for quality writing not found on the best seller lists and most book stores, Munro's books will be the perfect place to find a new author you can stuff into your backpack or ease into during the flight home.

Ditch Records

784 Fort St., Victoria, BC, V8W 1H2, Canada
250-386-5874
http://www.ditchrecords.com/

It's strange to have a kid ask, "What's a CD?" There are those of a certain age who remember when CD's were the stuff of science fiction and that music could only be found on vinyl LP's. While there are occasional attempts to bring out a new record on vinyl, those beloved records have gone the way of the Delorean. Music aficionados will swear that the sound of a pristine LP is far superior and richer than that of a CD. That is up for debate but what is not is the fact that many albums did not make the transition to the electronic age.

Some great albums that did not crack the best seller list have faded into obscurity, garage sales and shops like Ditch Records. If you're looking for a collection of Ringo Starr 45's or a genre bending Miles Davis album, you will find it at Ditch Records. It's a great place to shop for music old and new. You never know, you just may find that album your older brother had that you've not heard in nearly 30 years.

Silk Road Tea

1624 Government St.
Victoria, BC
V8W 1Z3
Canada
http://www.silkroadteastore.com/

In a city that prides itself on its British heritage, it is fitting one of the finest teashops this side of the Atlantic is found in Victoria. There are dozens, if not hundreds, of varieties of tea for sale. Everything from Alchemists Brew Herbal Tea to Yunnan Black tea can be found. A tea bar is available for you to relax with a cup of tea or indulge in tea tasting.

All manner of items used for brewing and drinking tea can be found. There is even an award-winning organic spa where you can get a massage. The website is a great place to find a recipe. If you're in Victoria and looking for a place to revive your road-weary soul, a cup or two of exotic tea at the Silk Road Tea shop may be just what you're looking for.

Manufactured by Amazon.ca
Acheson, AB